fushigi yûgi

The Mysterious Play
VOL. 1: PRIESTESS

FUSHIGI YUGI
THE MYSTERIOUS PLAY
VOL. 1: PRIESTESS
SHÔJO EDITION

This volume contains the FUSHIGI YÛGI installments from Animerica Extra Vol. 1, No. 1, through Vol. 2, No. 4, in their entirety.

STORY AND ART BY YUU WATASE

English Adaptation/Yuji Oniki
Translation Assist/Kaori Kawakubo Inoue
Touch-up & Lettering/Andy Ristaino
Cover Design/Hidemi Sahara
Graphics & Design/Hidemi Sahara
Editor/William Flanagan
Shôjo Edition Editor/Elizabeth Kawasaki

Editor in Chief, Books/Alvin Lu
Editor in Chief, Magazines/Marc Weidenbaum
VP of Publishing Licensing/Rika Inouye
VP of Sales/Gonzalo Ferreyra
Sr. VP of Marketing/Liza Coppola
Publisher/Hyoe Narita

Printed in Canada

Published by VIZ Media, LLC
P.O. Box 77010
San Francisco, CA 94107

1st English edition published 1999

Shôjo Edition
10 9 8 7 6 5
First printing, October 2003
Fifth printing, February 2008

www.viz.com
store.viz.com

fushigi yûgi

The Mysterious Play
VOL. 1: PRIESTESS

Story & Art By
YUU WATASE

CONTENTS

MODERN JAPAN
AND A CHINA THAT NEVER WAS

The story of FUSHIGI YÛGI ("The Mysterious Play") takes place in two different worlds—present-day Japan and a version of ancient China that can be found in the romantic Chinese epics.

The main character of our story, Miaka, is a junior-high-school student who, like every other Japanese student her age, must pass a difficult test to enter the school of her choice. The better a reputation the school has, the harder the entrance exam. For that purpose, students in their third and final year of junior high become very serious about their studies and not only engulf themselves in their school work, but also go to evening "cram schools" where they take even more classes directed at passing their examinations.

The fantasy world of the book, THE UNIVERSE OF THE FOUR GODS, is based on classics of Chinese literature such as THE ROMANCE OF THE THREE KINGDOMS and many other tales of adventure and magic written nearly two-thousand years ago. It is an age where warring states vie for control of the most advanced civilization in the ancient world, and young emperors have inherited regimes that have been passed down from their forefathers in an unbroken line spanning thousands of years. It is a world of beauty and danger, and to enter, you have but to turn the page....

THE UNIVERSE OF THE FOUR GODS is based on ancient China, but Japanese pronunciation of Chinese names differs slightly from their Chinese equivalents. Here is a short glossary of the Japanese pronunciation of the Chinese names in this graphic novel:

Chinese	Japanese	Person or Place	Meaning
Xong Gui-Siu	Sô Kishuku	Tamahome's name	Demon Constellation
Hong-Nan	Konan	Southern Kingdom	Crimson South
Gong Wu	Kyûbu	A clue	Palace Strength
Tai Yi-Jun	Tai Itsukun	An oracle	Preeminent Person
Kang-Lin	Kôrin	A lady of Hong-Nan	Peaceful Jewel
Daichi-San	Daikyokuzan	A mountain	Greatest Mountain

HOTOHORI
A beautiful noble of ancient China who lives in the palace

TAMAHOME
A dashing miser from ancient China

YUI
Miaka's best friend and a very intelligent girl who is certain to get into Jonan High School easily

MIAKA
A chipper, middle-school glutton who is trying to get into the exclusive Jonan High School to please her mother

KANG-LIN
An amazingly strong prospective bride for the emperor of the country of Hong-Nan in ancient China

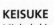

KEISUKE
Miaka's kind, college-student brother

MIAKA'S MOM
A divorced, single mother who is trying to see that her children receive the best education available

CHAPTER ONE
THE YOUNG LADY OF LEGENDS

DIING DOOONG

...A DREAM!!

WELL, WHADDAYA KNOW...

JEEZ... I GOT INTO TROUBLE *BIG* TIME.

WHAT'D YOU EXPECT? WE'VE GOT ENTRANCE EXAMS THIS SPRING, AND YOU'RE DRIFTING OFF IN CLASS.

BEEP!

TALK OR EAT! MAKE UP YOUR MIND!

UMPH AH HAVENT TOH ANYUN WET HUT-- (I HAVEN'T TOLD ANYONE YET BUT--)

THAT'S RIGHT. AREN'T YOU TRYING TO GET INTO YOTSUBADAI HIGH SCHOOL?

13

YOU AND YOUR G.P.A. SHOULD HAVE A MEETING OF THE MINDS.

THAT'S JONAN HIGH SCHOOL! THE TOP SCHOOL IN THE CITY!!

WHY DIDN'T YOU TELL YUI? SHE'S TAKING THE EXAM FOR JONAN.

CHOMP CHOMP

...

THE SCHOOL THAT ISSUES THAT UNIFORM?

ARE YOU *REALLY* MY BEST FRIEND!?

WELL, NO WONDER. I'M THE GENIUS AND SHE'S THE DUNCE.

OBVIOUSLY

NOPE! GOT CRAM SCHOOL TO ATTEND! I'M NOT HUNGRY ANYWAY! YOU FINISH IT OFF!

SEE YA

MIAKA, AREN'T YOU GOING TO EAT ANYMORE?

HEY YUI, I NEED TO COPY YOUR NOTES FROM PART OF TODAY'S CLASS THAT I SLEPT THROUGH.

HEEE!

RRRUMBLE

WHUD

MIAKA, CRAM SCHOOL WILL BE STARTING SOON!

WHAT'S THIS ROOM HERE??

SOME KIND OF EARTH-QUAKE!?!

HEY! LOOK AT THIS, YUI!

WE COULD MAKE A KILLING SELLING THIS STUFF.

LOOK AT ALL THESE BOOKS. THEY LOOK PRETTY RARE.

OWW! IF THIS IS A DREAM, IT'S A DREAM THAT *HURTS*!

THEN WHERE ARE WE?!?

'COURSE IT DOES!!

...DOES THIS HURT??

IS FOOD ALL YOU EVER THINK ABOUT?!?

OKAY, I CAN HANDLE THE LIBRARY BEING GONE. BUT THERE'S NO HÄAGEN DAZS, MISTER DONUTS, OR DENNY'S HERE!

WHMPP

22

24

WHAT? YOU'RE BROKE !?!

URK

WE USED IT UP AT THE BURGER JOINT.

WE DON'T HAVE A CENT.

HUH?

SKIP THE THANKS. I'LL TAKE THE MONEY!

POOR FOLKS BUG ME!

LATER!!

NOBODY ASKED YOU TO SAVE US!

DON'T YOU LADIES KNOW THAT MONEY MAKES THE WORLD GO AROUND?!?

TSK TSK TSK

I'M NOT GIVING OUT ANY FREE RIDES!

W-WAIT! WHERE ARE WE...

MIAKA! IT'S ANOTHER EARTH-QUAKE!!

Hello. It's me, Watase, and I'll be using this space to chat a little. I know, I know. You're complaining about my bad handwriting, sorry but I just scribble stuff down. (Bad handwriting approximated for the English edition – ed.) I don't like writing by hand. But since my writing is difficult enough to read I've decided to take some pains to write more legibly. Yeah right.

Now let's see, "Fushigi Yûgi"... when I was eighteen, before I got published, I looked up this incredibly thick "Buddhist Philosophy Encyclopedia" and was delighted to find how the character for "Oni" was read as "Tamahome." I discovered that "when the light of the Tamahome star in Suzaku's seven southern star constellations (out of a total of 28 constellations) fades, it is a sign of a bad harvest." As I came across this information, I came up with the idea for this story. I thought up the characters of Tamahome 鬼宿, and Hotohori 星宿, but Miaka still wasn't part of the picture. (I wanted to use the character for star rather than constellation which would make Tamahome 鬼星 (pronounced Kisei) but that would have made Hotohori 星星 (pronounced Seisei) so I decided against it). I submitted the "FY" story idea along with my "Shishunki Miman Okotowari" (No Interest in Prepubescence) idea. "Shishunki" was accepted instead of "FY."

Although I've done my share of research on China for this story, it's still not a Chinese story. "FY" departs significantly from some basic historical facts. So please don't read it as if it were Chinese history. Who would? (For example, the emperor calls himself "Chin" so I decided against him using his real name.) I just want to let you know that I haven't been delinquent in my research. I read through 10 books before I began working on this serial. If there are any discrepancies, they're being made with my knowledge.

ALL RIGHT! YOU HAVE TWO MONTHS TILL YOUR ENTRANCE EXAMS!!

THIS IS WHERE THE GOING GETS TOUGH. WILL YOU BE LAUGHING OR CRYING THIS SPRING? IT'S ALL DECIDED HERE!

YOU THINK YOU CAN GET INTO JONAN? YOU'LL HAVE TO BE IN THE TOP 75 PERCENTILE OR YOU WON'T STAND A CHANCE!

HARD LOVE

ONLY 30% OF THE APPLICANTS GET ACCEPTED! DO YOU STILL THINK THIS SPRING'S GOING TO BE A CAKEWALK? HMM?

THAT WAS TOO *WEIRD* TO BE A DREAM.

MAYBE IT WAS A HALLUCI-NATION CAUSED BY EXAM ANXIETY. DOUBTFUL.

WAA KKK

SO NOT ONLY ARE YOU LATE, BUT YOU'RE *DAY-DREAMING* TOO, EH, MIAKA?

"ALL RIGHT! YOU HAVE TWO MONTHS TILL YOUR ENTRANCE EXAMS!!"

"NEVER RUIN YOUR MORALE BY WHINING ABOUT HOW YOU'RE GOING TO FAIL!"

"LISTEN CAREFULLY! DAICHU PREP SCHOOL HAS *NEVER* TURNED OUT A STUDENT WHO FAILED THEIR EXAMS."

I'LL BET YOU DIDN'T HEAR A WORD I SAID!

"THIS IS WHERE THE GOING GETS TOUGH. WILL YOU BE LAUGHING OR CRYING THIS SPRING? IT'S ALL DECIDED HERE!"

ALWAYS THE SAME STUPID SPEECH!

"EVERYONE ELSE TAKING THE EXAM IS YOUR ENEMY! KILL OR BE KILLED! THIS IS WAR" --

HUMPH! AND THE NIGHT BEFORE THE TEST, YOU CAN ALWAYS PRAY!

THA- THAT'S ENOUGH!!

I WISH THERE WAS A GOD I COULD PRAY TO!

IT'S NOT LIKE I'M TAKING THE JONAN EXAM 'CAUSE I WANT TO.

GIMME ANOTHER.

YOUR TEST SCORES ARE IN FROM THE LAST TRIAL EXAM, MIAKA.

SPUTTZ

YOU'RE DOING BETTER BUT *STILL* NOT GOOD ENOUGH FOR JONAN.

NOW I WOULDN'T TELL YOU EVEN IF I KNEW.

NOPE... I KNOW ABOUT THE FOUR GODS, THO.

WELL, TODAY AT THE LIBRARY...

JEEZ! THAT'S YOUR *THIRD* BOWL. WHERE DO YOU PUT IT ALL?

!?

HEY, YOU'RE MAJORING IN CHINESE PHILOSOPHY, RIGHT? YOU EVER HEAR OF "THE UNIVERSE OF THE FOUR GODS"?

32

OF COURSE!!

HA HA HA HA HA

YOU'LL BE JUST FINE, I *KNOW* YOU'LL DO IT FOR ME, RIGHT?

UMM... MOM, YOTSUBADAI IS REALLY WHERE...

GOTTA FINISH THIS DIARY ENTRY AND GET BACK TO STUDYING. "FOUND A STRANGE BOOK IN THE LIBRARY..." AND...

OOPS!

PASS YOUR EN- TRANCE EXAM!!

AND THEN...

YOU'VE GROWN INTO SUCH A FINE YOUNG WOMAN! AS A SINGLE PARENT, YOU'RE MAKING ME PROUD!

AAARR-RRGH! MY ARM!

STOP IT!!

ギリッ

ARE YOU ALL RIGHT, MY LOVELY?

OH, YES. ♥

HE WAS TALL AND KINDA GOOD-LOOKING.

BUT A MONEY-GRUBBER.

THAT BOY IN MY DREAM... HE HAD THE CHINESE CHARACTER FOR DEMON WRITTEN ON HIS FOREHEAD.

WHOOPS! GOTTA STUDY TO KEEP MOM HAPPY!

BONG BONG

then i met someone who was too greedy, but god was he gorgeous!! ♥

MIAKA, I'VE BROUGHT YOU A SNACK.

URP

34

37

38

41

HOW'D I GET TO THE LIBRARY ??

I DID IT ALL JUST TO MAKE YOU HAPPY.

CITY CENTRAL LIBRARY

I WONDER IF YUI CAME TODAY...

RESTRICTED PRIVATE LIBRARY

KREEK

チョロ チョロ

THE LIBRARIAN ISN'T HERE.

43

SO YOU READ THIS BOOK TO THE END, AND YOU GET A WISH, HMM?

WHEN PIGS FLY. BUT I MIGHT AS WELL JUST KILL SOME TIME READING IT.

THE BOOK... IT'S STILL OPEN.

I'LL STAY HERE! A LITTLE WORRYING WILL DO MOM GOOD!

GAK

WHY'D I JUST THINK OF *HIM*? HE WAS JUST A *DREAM*.

I WISH I HAD A GOOD-LOOKING BOY-FRIEND...

I WISH MY PROBLEMS WOULD DISAPPEAR -- PROBLEMS WITH THE ENTRANCE EXAMS... PROBLEMS WITH MOM...

I WISH I WERE PRETTY, SMART AND POPULAR WITH THE BOYS, LIKE YUI...

44

And thus the young lady of legends opened the door to another world, and likewise began our tale.

CHAPTER TWO
THE BOY WITH THE DEMON STAR

Fushigi Yûgi ～ 1

HM?

WHAT AM--

WHA--

WHAT'LL I DO? WHAT'LL I DO? WHAT'LL I DO??

I'VE GOT TO GET BACK HOME!

THAT'S RIGHT! I WAS AT THE LIBRARY, READING "THE UNIVERSE OF THE FOUR GODS"...

...AND I WAS SUCKED INTO THE BOOK!!

OH...

THE LAST TIME I WAS HERE WITH YUI, WE MADE IT BACK, NO PROBLEM, NO WORRIES.

GO FER BROKE! I'LL JUST STAY HERE!

CAN'T GO HOME AFTER THAT FIGHT WITH MOM!

OKAY, MIAKA, WHAT ARE YOU GONNA DO WHEN YOU GET BACK?

ガラ ガラ

ガラ

NOW THAT I'VE DECIDED THAT...

ガラガラ トン

THERE AIN'T NOBODY THAT HANDSOME BACK HOME!

AND SINCE I'M HERE ANYWAY, I'LL FIND THAT BOY!

IT LOOKS LIKE A MOVIE SET!!

WOW!

I'M IMPRESSED!!

IT'S HIM!!

EX-CUSE ME...

Y'O   Y'O

HUH ??

HEY...

52

54

IS THAT *TRUE*??

WOAH !

I HEARD THIS RUMOR THAT SHE WAS LOOKING FOR SOME BOY WITH A DEMON ON HIS FOREHEAD.

NEVER HEARD OF 'IM.

AS LONG AS YOU PAY, I'LL DO JUST ABOUT ANYTHING.

IS SHE A GIRL IN A SHORT SKIRT WITH HER HAIR DONE IN BUNS, OR DID SHE HAVE SHORT HAIR?

HOW WOULD I KNOW?

WHO'RE YOU ANYWAY ??

OH! I'M SORRY. IF YOU'LL TAKE ONE OF THESE. MY CARD.

JACK-OF-ALL-TRADES?

So I just want to clarify some things about my background. It seems I have to inform every reader that I'm a woman. 😊 As for how old I am...because I'm pretty young I'm not embarrassed about my age. Suffice to say I first got published at 18 and then "Prepubescence" came out when I was 20. You do the math.

I've had fans who tell me, "I want to be a manga artist just like you." Don't be just like me! "Lately I've been copying your drawings so much they look like yours." Well I suppose that's all right as long as you eventually acquire your own style. Every artist is always influenced by somebody else in the beginning. But I don't think it's such a good idea to continue copying other artists after you get published. Although they may seem the same, there's a big difference between being a big fan of an artist and unconsciously resembling that style, or parody, or reference, and PLAGIARISM. Lifting one or two ideas or scenes I can handle, but if you make a comic exactly like mine, I'll get mad at you!

I dunno, uh...

all of a sudden | Watase's current state

Now THAT"S something that can get me mad! (I'm still new to this.) I know that there are tons of ideas that resemble each other, but to steal an episode verbatim... and when I get upset it means I'm 10 times angrier than the average person. (Usually I'm laid back no matter what people say to me. Friends will say, "Why don't you get mad once in awhile," and get mad at me!) Guess I haven't grown up. For the past two years, I haven't read any of my favorite manga artists who have influenced me! (Actually I haven't been reading much manga in general.) I want to shed my influences. I just want to draw manga my own way. But my drawings aren't getting better! And I'm working on it so hard!

YOU'RE STILL BROKE, RIGHT?

すたすたすた

THANK ME?

YOU'VE SAVED ME TWICE. I FEEL LIKE I OWE YOU.

たたっ

TO THANK YOU! THAT'S IT! I WANTED TO THANK YOU!!

LIS-TEN YOU...

I CAN'T GO HOME AFTER THAT BIG FIGHT WITH MY MOM.

DON'T SWEAT IT. I'VE GOT WORK TO DO, SO DON'T COME FOLLOW-ING ME.

GO ON HOME!

I COULDN'T EVEN IF I WANTED TO.

I DON'T WANT TO BE ALONE.

...

SKRICH
SKRICH—

PLEASE
PLEASE
PLEASE

LOOK, YOU CAN'T KEEP HANGING ALL OVER ME LIKE THIS!

BUT IF I HELP YOU IN YOUR WORK, IT'S OKAY, RIGHT?!?

IF YOU COULD FETCH A COUPLE OF GEMS FROM THE EMPEROR'S CROWN, I'D BE ROLLING IN MONEY.

BUT SINCE THAT'S IMPOSSIBLE, I'LL JUST BE MOSEYING ALONG...

IF YOU'RE THAT DETERMINED...

YOU SEE THAT FANCY PROCESSION OVER THERE! THAT'S FOR THE EMPEROR.

THE ONE IN THE CENTER IN THE GAUDIEST CARRIAGE IS THE EMPEROR OF HONG-NAN.

68

WHA--?

HE'S YOUNG!

I NEED YOU TO DO ME A FAVOR!

...

I'D REALLY APPRECIATE IT IF YOU COULD SPARE ME TWO GEMS FROM YOUR CROWN.

WHO IS THIS ??

HEY! ARE YOU THE EMPEROR ?!?

NO ONE IS RUDE TO THE EMPER-OR!!

HEY!

UMM...

...

SOMEBODY SAVED MY LIFE AND I GOTTA PAY HIM BACK! YOU CAN SPARE THEM! WHAT'S THE PROBLEM? HOLD ON A SEC!

QUIT BEING SO PRISSY! IT AIN'T LIKE YOU'RE SOME DEBUTANTE!

KILL HER!!

71

THERE THEY ARE!!

BASTARD! YOU'LL *PAY* FOR THAT!!

!?

BLUSH

UNDER THE EMPEROR'S ORDERS, TAMAHOME AND THE YOUNG LADY WERE IMPRISONED IN THE BASEMENT DUNGEON OF THE PALACE.

HEY KEISUKE, WHERE'S DADDY?

MIAKA, MOM AND DAD ARE *DIVORCED*.

DIVORST?

MOM ...

DON'T BE SAD...

BUT I *AM* SO SAD!

SO DON'T LOOK SO SAD...

I'D DO ANYTHING TO MAKE YOU HAPPY, MOMMY.

IT'S YOU, TAMAHOME! YOU *SCARED* ME!

YOU'RE SCARED? I'M TERRIFIED!

THERE YOU ARE, SNOOZING LIKE A BABY...

...WHILE WE'RE *LOCKED* IN THE PALACE DUNGEON!

"I'M FROM ANOTHER WORLD, AND I WAS SUCKED INTO SOME BOOK I FOUND IN THE LIBRARY."

YEAH, LIKE HE'LL BUY THAT.

WHAT'LL I TELL HIM? "WE'RE IN A BOOK."

WHAT WAS THAT LIGHT COMING OUT OF YOUR BODY!?

WHERE'RE YOU FROM, ANY-WAY?

......SKTCH SKTCH

BUT IT LOOKS LIKE I CAN GO BACK AND FORTH BETWEEN WORLDS AS LONG AS THE BOOK'S OPEN.

......

SO WHAT'S UP WITH YOUR MOM? YOU WERE TOSSING IN YOUR SLEEP!

WELL, WHAT-EVER.

WHY HAVE YOU NOT PUT THEM TO DEATH YET!?!

ESPECIALLY THAT BIZARRE WOMAN! SHE EMITTED THAT STRANGE LIGHT AND ATTEMPTED TO VANISH!

SHE MIGHT BE AN EVIL SPIRIT, YOUR MAJESTY! NOW, WITH YOUR PERMISSION...

WE HAVE CAUSE TO WONDER...

...IF THAT GIRL MIGHT BE THE YOUNG LADY OF LEGENDS.

ONE MOMENT.

☙ Priestess ❧

Getting back to where we left off, I'm sure some of my work reminds the readers of other comics. Of course I never do it consciously! (Even I have some pride). Someone ends up pointing it out, and then I'm like "oh my god!" wait. "Magical Nan" ♪ was different. That came from a book my editor gave me. Although I tried to make my version totally different, due to limitations on the number of pages, I was told to imitate the book. I really do try not to copy scenes. During junior high and high school I was influenced mostly by people like Toyoo Ashida (director, animation director: Yamato, Minky Momo and Vampire Hunter D) and Akemi Takada (character designer: Creamy Mami, Urusei Yatsura, Kimagure Orange Road) (My older drawings from "Prepubescence Vol. 3", I was really into Takada at the time) and Mutsumi Inomata (character designer: Windaria, Leda, Brain-Powerd), anime artists rather than comic artists. Now I hardly get a chance to watch animation at all, so I don't know what's going on these days. I really loved animation. Seems so long ago. I tried to cram these animation influences into a shōjo manga drawing style that never really existed before. (I've asked many people, and there's nobody else who draws like I do).

It's really hard to find a balance. I have many fellow artists who can give me advice, but I just can't change at this point.

I think that my own pictures are too complicated! I was really into boys' comics so everyone thought I'd be writing for shonen manga magazines such as Shonen Sunday. But can you believe that maybe after three years of hard work, I finally managed to draw shōjo manga effectively? ♥ I still have a long way to go. Okay, okay, I'm getting a little long-winded here but most of my fan letters come from people who want to become comic artists, so you guys can use this as a reference (maybe). To sum up, I recommend you study and incorporate all the elements of artists you admire in your unique way into your own drawings (without ripping them off). I tend to discard those elements that don't fit with my style. You should also read as many novels, see as many films and dramas as possible. Remember the great Osamu Tezuka once said, "If you want to write a new manga then don't bother reading another manga!" Of course, this is coming from someone who bought his "How To Draw Manga" AFTER getting published! Sorry!

My friends razzed me about it. But I don't know how to do effects work. So sue me!! ♪

93

98

OUR APOLOGIES. TRICKERY WAS NOT OUR INTENTION.

WE SIMPLY WISHED TO UNDERSTAND YOU BETTER.

HE SEEMS LIKE A COMPLETELY DIFFERENT PERSON.

SITTING LIKE THIS IS KILLING ME.

OKAY~

SO THEN... YOU'RE GONNA LET US GO?

AT LEASE WE'VE DISPROVED OUR COUNSELOR'S ASSERTION THAT YOU ARE EVIL SPIRITS.

AHEM

OF COURSE, YOU SHALL NOT BE EXECUTED.

HAVE YOU CONSIDERED RULING THE WORLD?

˜CHUCKLE˜ YOU'RE MUCH TOO MODEST.

THIS YOUNG LADY WILL OBTAIN THE POWER OF SUZAKU

THE PRIESTESS OF SUZAKU, THE ONE WHO WILL PROTECT OUR EMPIRE, STANDS BEFORE YOU!

EVERYONE, STAND BACK!!

ざわっ

I'M THERE! I'LL DO IT! I'LL BE YOUR PRIESTESS OF SUZAKU !!

MY LIFE HAS BEEN LEADING UP TO THIS!!

I-IS THAT SO?

WATCH IT!

YOU'RE MAKIN' TOO MUCH OF THIS!

HOPE I DON'T DISAPPOINT.

PLEASE LOOK AFTER TAMAHOME FOR ME!

OKAY. AND NOW I'LL BE HEADING ON HOME!

SEE YA!

EVEN TAMAHOME'S BOWING!

THEY'RE TREATING ME LIKE I'M ALL HIGH AND MIGHTY!

WELL, YEAH... BUT FIRST I GOTTA APOLOGIZE TO MY MOM.

WHAT ARE YOU TALKING ABOUT? YOU JUST SAID...

AND I HAVE SCHOOL.

WELL... AT LEAST MY WORRIES OVER MY ENTRANCE EXAMS ARE OVER!

HEY! WHAT'S THIS BOOK DOING ON THE FLOOR?

CHAPTER FOUR
THE SEVEN
CONSTELLATIONS
OF SUZAKU

I MAY NEVER SEE TOKYO AGAIN!!

THE BOOKSTORE NEAR THE STATION WHERE WE'D ALWAYS HANG OUT...

KAWAHARA BOOKSTORE

SCHOOL ... MY CLASS-MATES ...

EVEN THAT HORRIBLE CRAM SCHOOL.

I DID IT! I FORCED HER OUT 'OF THE HOUSE!!

→ HOW THE WORLD WORKS IN MIAKA'S IMAGINATION.

NOW OUR UPDATE ON THE MISSING JUNIOR HIGH SCHOOL GIRL. EXAM PRESSURE IS REPORTED TO BE THE CAUSE...

HOW MANY DAYS HAS IT BEEN SINCE I CAME, HERE? I BET RIGHT NOW...

111

I'M STILL ALIVE!!

HEY!

SNIFF SNIFF

SNIFF

DON'T BURY ME YET!

WE WERE SUPPOSED TO GO TO HIGH SCHOOL TOGETHER!

AND THEN EVENTUALLY...

MIAKA, WHY, WHY DID YOU HAVE TO...

WHAT EVER SHALL I DO ABOUT *UNDER-WEAR!?*

A TRUE TRAGEDY.

AND... AND...

YOU MAKE SOME GREAT FACES!

T-TAMA-HOME! HOW DARE YOU SNEAK INTO MY ROOM!!

C'MON! I'M HERE TO CHEER YOU UP! HIS MAJESTY'S WORRIED ABOUT YOU, TOO.

114

MIAKA!

THAT'S RIGHT!

I'M SORRY. I'VE BEEN SO BUSY...

...I COULDN'T SPEND ANY TIME WITH YOU.

I WAS RESEARCHING THAT IN "THE UNIVERSE OF THE FOUR GODS."

SAY, I WAS WONDERING HOW I COULD OBTAIN THE POWERS OF THE SUZAKU.

"U-U-UNIVERSE OF THE FOUR GODS"!? THAT'S THE BOOK WE'RE *IN*!

YES, IT'S A BOOK OF PROPHECIES HANDED DOWN FROM TAI YI-JUN TO HIS MAJESTY TAI JU.*

OH NO, NOT AT ALL, HOTOHORI ... I MEAN, YOUR MAJESTY!

115   *THE FIRST EMPEROR OF HOTOHORI'S DYNASTY.

IN THE BOOK, THERE ARE 28 HOLY CONSTELLATIONS OF HEAVEN (THE 28 CELESTIALS). EACH OF THE FOUR CARDINAL POINTS, NORTH, SOUTH, EAST, AND WEST, CLAIMS SEVEN CONSTELLA- TIONS.

THE SOUTHERN SEVEN CONSTELLATIONS ARE CALLED "THE SUZAKU." IT'S A GENERAL ASTRONOMICAL TERM.

AND I THOUGHT IT WAS SOME KINDA GOD OF BIRDS.

THE NAMES OF THE SEVEN CONSTELL- ATIONS ARE...

CHICHIRI TAMAHOME
井 鬼
NURIKO HOTOHORI CHIRIKO
柳 星 張
TASUKI MITSUKAKE
翼 軫

THEY MAKE UP THE SOUTHERN SEVEN CONSTELLATIONS, SUZAKU.

THAT'S CORRECT.

TAMAHOME AND HOTOHORI !?

...THE PRIESTESS OF SUZAKU SO THAT SHE CAN OBTAIN HER MAGICAL POWERS.

I, HOTOHORI (HYDRA), AND TAMAHOME (CANCER), AND THE REST OF THE SEVEN CONSTELLATIONS MUST PROTECT ...

OH, MY!

A SHOCKED TAMAHOME SUDDENLY APPEARS.

WHAT IS THIS? SOME ROLE-PLAYING GAME!?

GET A GRIP

YOU MUST FIND THE OTHER FIVE. UNLESS YOU PERSONALLY GATHER ALL SEVEN YOU WILL NOT OBTAIN THE POWERS OF SUZAKU.

SAYS SO RIGHT HERE.

ACCORDING TO THE BOOK, THE YOUNG LADY WHO GATHERS TOGETHER THE "SEVEN CONSTELLATIONS OF SUZAKU" WILL HAVE HER EVERY WISH GRANTED.

S-SO THEN ... THERE ARE FIVE OTHER PEOPLE WHO HAVE SIGNS APPEARING ON THEIR BODIES!?

I KNEW MY NAME CAME FROM A CONSTELLATION, BUT... SO I'M SUPPOSED TO PROTECT YOU, HUH??

DID YOU KNOW ABOUT THIS, TAMAHOME!?!

IN LESS THAN THREE MONTHS I HAVE TO TAKE MY HIGH SCHOOL ENTRANCE EXAMS!!

UH-OH!

NO WONDER... THEY'VE BEEN SO KIND TO ME.

IF I DON'T FIND THE OTHER FIVE BY THEN...

HELD BACK

HOLD ON. THERE'S A CLUE IN THE BOOK. AREN'T YOU LISTENING??

NO WAY!, WHERE ART THOU, CONSTELLATION NUMBER THREE??

THE THIRD CONSTELLATION IS REFERRED TO BY THE CHARACTERS GONG AND WU. THE FIRST ONE MEANS PALACE AND THE SECOND MEANS FIERCE STRENGTH.

宮

武

SO WHEN WE FIND THE MOST VALIANT MAN IN THE PALACE, WE'LL HAVE FOUND THE THIRD OF OUR SEVEN CONSTELLA-TIONS.

AS INSTRUCTED, WE HAVE SELECTED THE FINEST WARRIORS IN THE PALACE.

YOUR MAJESTY, YOUR EMINENCE,

IT DOESN'T APPEAR BECAUSE THE GUY WANTS IT TO.

HE MIGHT NOT EVEN KNOW HE'S GOT IT.

LET ME GIVE 'EM A LITTLE TEST.

DO ANY OF YOU HAVE CHARAC-TERS THAT APPEAR ON YOUR BODY?

AHEM

WELL DONE.

TAMAHOME... OUR PURPOSE WAS *NOT* TO ALLOW YOU TO SHOW OFF.

HUH ??

ぴた

HMM

LOOKS LIKE IT'S MY TURN.

WH- WHAT TH-

DODGEBALL

AND WHAT MIGHT YOU HAVE IN MIND?

I'LL BE FINE! THE ONLY THING MY TEACHERS EVER COMPLIMENTED ME ON WAS MY SPEED!

MIAKA, TRY TO *CATCH* IT FOR ONCE!

SHE'S THE ONLY ONE LEFT.

HUFF HUFF

SCHOOL COMPETITIONS

1

DOESN'T THAT JUST PROVE THAT YOU'RE A GLUTTON ??

121

IN THE SAME WAY BRAVE DOGS DON'T BARK TOO MUCH. WATCH.

BESIDES, A TRULY VALIANT MAN WOULD NEVER TOUCH A GIRL.

AND WHO IS THE MAN NEXT TO THEM?

WHY IS SHE SO *FRIENDLY* WITH HIS MAJESTY? SHE'S NO EMPRESS!

KANG-LIN, WE HAVE TO GO BACK!

WE'LL BE SCOLDED FOR BEING HERE!

HE IS ONE OF THE PROTECTORS OF THE PRIESTESS. A CELESTIAL WARRIOR OF SUZAKU, TAMAHOME.

SNEEK

SO THAT'S THE PRIESTESS OF SUZAKU EVERYONE'S BEEN TALKING ABOUT?

122

124

125

TAMA... HOME...?

ALL THE WARRIORS ARE UNCONSCIOUS.

WE DON'T HAVE ENOUGH PEOPLE TO MOVE IT...

SO THAT WAS YOU...

FOR A MOMENT I FELT SOMETHING COVERING ME...

TAMA-HOME! YOU'LL BE CRUSHED! STOP IT!

131

Let me just say that drawing the buildings in this chapter was no easy task. I did all this research to draw them (although I didn't want it to look exactly the same as in my reference, so I'd alter some of the designs and layouts). It was a real pain for my assistants but also for me as well. (I do as much of the backgrounds as I possibly can.) Hey, Chinese architecture, why're you such a pain!? And these outfits are no easier. Not to mention the mob scenes. And I've had it up to here with the soldiers' armor! (I'm gonna use "Romance of the Three Kingdoms" as reference material, but that story's set too far back in time. ♪ There's not a whole lot of changes over time in China but we're talking about a difference of a thousand years. ♪ At least I want the armor to be right. The armor is kind of a pastiche between different periods, mostly the period between the Sung and Ming dynasties but also a little bit of Tang all mixed up together. But this China is supposed to be a work of the imagination. Even my editor's been telling me not to be too particular.

When I was in elementary school, I loved the TV live drama show "Saiyuki." Then they started doing re-runs when I was eighteen. All of a sudden I realized how great the action, characters, and comedy were. So I'd look forward to 8 p.m. every Sunday. That's really the kind of project I'd like to work on.

By the way, I really wanted to have Tamahome wear an outfit with Chinese buttons, but the style only came into existence in modern China. I might eventually draw it in anyway. In the first graphic novel, maybe! The kimono style just isn't much fun. When were the "Mr. Vampire" and "Chinese Ghost Story" series set? I'd like Tamahome to wear the same clothes worn by the guy in "Mr. Vampire," but maybe that outfit would be too recent. I know, I know. I'm not supposed to be so particular, but I am. Oh, I also pay a lot of attention to hair. The bun style is just too boring.

YOUR EMINENCE, ARE YOU ALL RIGHT??

YOUR EMINENCE.

I THOUGHT MY HEART WOULD STOP, RIGHT THEN

TAMAHOME...

OUCH! TAKE IT EASY, WILL YA?

IS HE PROTECTING ME JUST BECAUSE I'M THE PRIESTESS OF SUZAKU?

THE POWER YOU DISPLAYED A MOMENT AGO, COULD THAT POSSIBLY BE....

HE DOESN'T KNOW BECAUSE HE'S NEVER BEEN THERE.

ARE YOU AN EMPIRIAL CONSORT FROM THE INNER SERAGLIO?

OR ...

I AM KANG-LIN. OR "NURIKO" AS IN THE CONSTELLATION.

BONGG

SO SHE'S A WOMAN!!

GREAT! WE'VE ALREADY FOUND THE THIRD CONSTELLATION....

THANK YOU FOR RESCUING ME!

I'M MIAKA YŪKI!!

LET'S SHAKE

CHAPTER FIVE
DANGEROUS LOVE

140

142

143

144

YOU'RE HURTING ME! DON'T PULL SO HARD!

DROP DROP DROP

RUBB RUBB RUBB

CLEAN IT UP. IF YOU MISS ANY SPOTS, YOU'LL GET *NO* DINNER.

IT'S *DUSTY* OUT HERE.

I'M SORRY! I LOST MY GRIP ...

THAT'S NOT FAIR ...!!

WHAT !?!

THAT'S THE DIRTIEST FLOOR I'VE EVER SEEN! NO DINNER FOR YOU!

ME!??

BOO HOO

HEY, QUIT PICKIN'... ON MIAKA. Y'KNOW, I JUST DON'T LIKE--

V-V-VERY DISTURB-ING BEHAVIOR....

TAMA-BABY, FORGET THE *USELESS* WENCH. LET'S GO HAVE DINNER ♥

TWITCH

TWITCH

GWUPH

KRAKLE KRAKLE

I'M SO HAPPY!

NOW, WAIT! I NEVER *SAID* I DIDN'T LIKE YOU!

YOU DON'T LIKE ME!! I'M NOT *GOOD* ENOUGH! YOU WANT THE LITTLE *FLAKE!* YOU WANT THE LITTLE *TWIT!*

THEN... THEN YOU *LIKE* ME!?

GRR GRR GRR GRR GRRGA

GRR-RRRRR

147

148

So I was reading some fan mail informing me that "Prepubescence" was voted second place in the top 20 manga poll of an anime magazine in Taiwan (I think). Can it really be true? A friend in the bookstore business told me that it was ranked in the top 10, 20, 30, or something. I dunno what it was, but I'm just happy to be ranked! Sniffl sniffl Thank you everyone, so much! I received some fan mail from Taiwan, from a 15-year-old named Li. So I have readers abroad! A girl who was half Chinese and half Japanese wrote me when I was working on "Treasure of the Heart," Yui Len (I could have the wrong spelling), and she's studying martial arts with a real master. That's awesome! Her name is so cute, I'll have to use it in a future manga. I once got a letter from someone who's half British/half Japanese... very international. I have to admit I'm a little nervous about having native Chinese reading "Fushigi Yûgi." Oh, and thanks so much for the tapes. I'm changing the subject. I listen to them all! There's B'z, TMN, Ranma soundtracks, recorded letters, Lodoss soundtracks, etc. Oh, when I mentioned COCO in "Prepubescence," I had lots of people writing back! They're really popular! A special thanks to the people who made compilation tapes of COCO songs dedicated to scenes in "Prepubescence." They were great! It's true that "Your Song, My Song" is really appropriate as Manato's song right around the "to live in the present" scene. "Melody" is perfect for the scene where Asuka is hiding in the rain, watching Manato. The best song though is "Circus Game"!! I was thinking how much I wanted it to be the theme song! But I found out that the "No Interest in Prepubescence" CD is coming out!! I'm on it too, so please listen to it. For those who are just now being introduced to my work, "No Interest in Prepubescence" is a three-volume comic. Check it out!! ♥

But why wasn't the COCO tune "Why?" on the tape. "Why?" Oh, I get it; just so I'd make a silly pun.

SO DO YOU LIKE NURIKO?

NO WAY! I ONLY MET HER YESTERDAY. BESIDES, SHE'S NOT MY TYPE.

I FEEL KINDA GUILTY.

NURIKO WOULD BE *FURIOUS* IF SHE SAW US LIKE THIS.

I GET IT.

I SEE!

(ははは)

REALLY? YOU HAVE *NO* FEELINGS WHAT-SO-EVER?

.....

I--

I'M NOT *JEA-LOUS*!!

...BUT MONEY IS MY FIRST LOVE.

HAHAHAHA

CAREFUL, GIRL. I'M A HEART-BREAKER!!

YOU'RE *JEALOUS!*

I REALIZE THAT I'M A KIND, MACHO, BEEFCAKE OF A MARTIAL ARTIST...

.....

HOPE YOU HAD A GOOD LAUGH

HA HA HA

...

OVER YOU.

I WAS JUST FEELING SORRY FOR NURIKO.

NOTH-ING MORE THAN THAT.

I WASN'T JEALOUS ...

WHAT IS IT? ALL OF THE SUDDEN.

MIAKA, COULD YOU COME OVER HERE?

SOME TIME AGO, I LOST A VERY PRECIOUS EARRING WHILE I WAS TAKING A WALK NEAR THE POND.

OH

HMF!

FOOL!

YOU WANT *ME* TO GO GET IT?

OH!

IT'S MADE OUT OF A CLEAR CRYSTAL ... SO IT'S HARD TO FIND!

THE JEWEL IS CALLED "GLOWSTONE" AND IT SHINES IN THE DARK. BUT THE POND IS SO DEEP AND MY ATTENDANTS ARE TOO SCARED TO FIND IT AT NIGHT...

OH, *WOULD* YOU!?

IN RETURN I PROMISE TO SERVE AS ONE OF THE SEVEN CELESTIAL WARRIORS OF SUZAKU.

AND, AS YOU KNOW, I AM NOT ALLOWED TO LEAVE THE INNER BUILDINGS!

I *SO* MISS THAT EAR-RING!

SURE! I'LL BE BACK IN A SEC.

153

THAT'LL TEACH HER...

DID YOU SAY WHAT I *THOUGHT* YOU SAID ...!?

...GONNA DROWN!!

DAMMIT!!

I AM *NOT*...

MIAKA
...

I DON'T LIKE HER. SHE'S GOT YOU AND THE EMPEROR WRAPPED AROUND HER LITTLE FINGER.

I'VE BEEN IN THE INNER SERAGLIO FOR A *YEAR* AND HE'S NEVER CAST A *GLANCE* IN MY DIRECTION!

I'LL *NEVER* LET GO! NOT SO YOU CAN RUN TO *HER*!!

L-- LEMME GO, YOU MUSCLE-BOUND BROAD!!

CLING CLING

MIAKA'S TRYING HER HARDEST JUST TO BE FRIENDS WITH YOU! DON'T YOU *SEE* THAT!?

164

CHAPTER SIX
HIDDEN LOVE

173

174

HEY, YOU CAN'T PUSH ME ARO--

OF COURSE, IT WILL NOT BE BY DECREE.

I'LL MAKE SURE *YOU* FALL IN LOVE WITH ME.

I-- I CAN'T BELIEVE THIS *!!*

WHO COULD STOP HIM?

DI-ING DO-NG

CHIRP CHIRP

NOT A WINK OF SLEEP.

HE JUST *PROPOSED* TO ME!!

DEEPLY TROUBLED

TAMAHOME HEARD ALL THAT. I WONDER WHAT HE'S THINKING...

WHAT AM I GONNA DO? DOESN'T HE REALIZE I HAVE TO GET OUT OF THIS BOOK AND TAKE MY ENTRANCE EXAMS?!

DOES THIS ALL HAPPEN IN THE BOOK? DOES SOME GORGEOUS GUY PROPOSE TO THE HEROINE?

YO...

UM

UM

WHADDLE I DO?

POING

I WILL NEVER FORGIVE YOU!!

IS *THIS* WHAT YOU MEAN BY "THERE'S NOTHING GOING ON BETWEEN HOTOHORI AND ME"?

IF HE'S GONNA BE *THAT* WAY...

A-AND I THOUGHT WE WERE ON THE VERGE OF BEING FRIENDS ...

TAMA-BABY, HOLD ON! I'M COMING WITH YOU! ♡

AND HOW COULD TAMAHOME GIVE ME THE COLD SHOULDER LIKE THAT *!?*

HE COULD HAVE SAID SOMETHING! DOESN'T HE CARE ABOUT ME*!?*

GRR

GRR

GRR

178

MAYBE ALL HE SEES ME AS IS AN OPPORTUNITY TO MAKE SOME MONEY.

TAMA-HOME...

WE'LL START THE BIDDING AT ONE SILVER RYO PER STICK

THAT'S TOO MUCH!

WHY WOULD YOU HAVE *ANYTHING* OF HER EMINENCE'S ??

THERE'S SOMETHING FISHY GOIN' ON HERE.

THAT'S RIGHT! THAT'S RIGHT!!

SOMEBODY COULDA SCRIBBLED WRITING ON THERE AND TRIED TO PASS IT OFF AS THE REAL THING!

WE JUST DON'T KNOW IF IT'S REAL!

HEY, YOU TRYING TO *SMEAR* MY TAMA-BABY!?

HMM...

I HEARD THE PRIESTESS LIVES IN THE *EMPEROR'S* PALACE!

181

182

185

186

!?

MAYBE MIAKA WENT BACK TO THE LIBRARY!

WHAT "BUSINESS"?

YOU WANNA WORK IN THIS TOWN, YOU GOTTA PAY FOR YOUR PROTECTION!

YOU JERKS! YOU THINK I GOT THAT KIND OF MONEY??

PLUS I LOST ALL MY GUM TO THAT CROWD.

188

Oops, my handwriting's getting sloppy again. Now here's something that caught me by surprise! I never thought you guys would like Tamahome with long hair!! When Tamahome's hair was trimmed shorter in this episode, the complaints came rushing in! I thought you'd prefer short hair, but boy was I wrong!! Tama's action scenes are hard to draw with his long hair. Don't worry, I'll never cut Hotohori's hair (My assistants and I call him "Ho-ri"). Apparently, the fans are divided between the Tamahome faction and Hotohori faction. I would never have believed your average junior high (and elementary) school student would be into Hotohori. Surprise! Which one will Miaka choose? I really can't portray a girl who can't decide on the guy she's in love with. I like a girl who's got her mind set on one guy. ♥ ♥ To say you like both guys equally only means that you aren't really in love with either of them. Although she herself might not even be aware of it. Well, let's not be too judgmental here.

I know I've said that I don't want any official fan club, but there are still people who want to join! Hmm, some people insisted on forming their own club and asked me how to let the entire country know about it. I got an idea! I'll print your address right here so everybody can see it! What do you think??

⟶ TA-DAHH.

Just kidding. You'd be so flooded with applications that you'd have a heart attack! (I'm not really that popular, though). ♪ Anyway, for your sake I won't mention it. Now, I heard there're people making their own Fushigi Yûgi dojinshi manga. That's okay, but be sure you send them to me too, okay? I'll be waiting to see them.♥

Until we meet again.

LISTEN, YOU TWO! YOUR PROTECTION RACKET IS GETTING OUTTA HAND. TAKE THIS AND SCRAM!

YOU ARE A MAN OF BUSINESS, RIGHT?

I'M IN THE BUSINESS OF TRADE FOR PROFIT, TOO.

THIS IS TROUBLE FOR MIAKA AND TAMA-BABY!

I'M SUCH A NICE PERSON, I'LL ACT AS A WITNESS! ♥

SHE'S BEING A MEANIE. →

GET A REAL FACE, MR. ♥ POTATO-CHIP HEAD!

Y-- YOU DARE TO INSULT ME!!

I'LL GIVE YOU A FULL THIRTY GOLD RYO FOR HER!

SELL ME THE GIRL!

191

194

TO BE CONTINUED IN VOLUME 2: ORACLE

The Fushigi Yûgi Guide to Sound Effects

Most of the sound effects in *FUSHIGI YÛGI* are the way Yû Watase created them, in their original Japanese.

We created this glossary for a page-by-page, panel-by-panel explanation of the action and background noises. By using this guide, you may even learn some Japanese.

The glossary lists the page number then panel. For example, 1.1 would indicate page 1, panel 1.

27.6	FX: ZUZU [earth shaking]
28.1	FX: GULAAAA [tree leaning over]
	FX: MEKI MEKI [tree breaking]
28.2	FX: SHIN [silence]
29.1	FX: BATAN [door slamming open]
31.1	FX: BESHI [slam]
34.2	FX: GILI [gripping hard]
35.2	FX: PAAA [car horn beeping]
36.2	FX: DOKUN DOKUN DOKUN DOKUN DOKUN [ba-dump ba-dump ba-dump ba-dump ba-dump]
	FX: DA [dashing off]
37.1	FX: KON KON [tap tap]
37.3	FX: PATAN [click]
38.1	FX: GUI [yank]
40.1	FX: PAN [smack]
41.3	FX: DON [shove]
42.1	FX: BATAAN [slam]
	FX: ZUZUZU [sliding down wall]
43.3	FX: KYOLO KYOLO [glance glance]
43.4	FX: KII [creak]
43.5	FX: PATAN [door closing softly]
44.2	FX: PETA [plop]
45.2-3	FX: DOKUN DOKUN DOKUN DOKUN DOKUN [ba-dump ba-dump ba-dump ba-dump]
46.1	FX: KA [flash of light]
46.3	FX: PINPON PINPON [bell chiming]
	FX: SAWA SAWA [people filing out]
47.1	FX: PALA PALA [flip flip]

**CHAPTER ONE:
THE YOUNG LADY OF LEGENDS**

10.3	FX: SU [bowl disappearing]
10.4	FX: SU [bowl disappearing]
11.1	FX: GATAN [desk bumping floor]
12.2	FX: DOKA DOKA [whack whack]
12.3	FX: PITA [stopping in place]
13.2	FX: PAPAAA BUOOO [car horns beeping]
13.3	FX: PAAA [car horn beeping]
15.3	FX: KALI KALI [scribble scribble]
16.3	FX: KOLO KOLO KOLO [roll roll roll]
16.4	FX: GII [creak]
17.5	FX: PALA PALA [flip flip]
19.1	FX: DOKA [whack]
19.3	FX: ZUZU [earth quaking]
	FX: ZUZUZUZU [bookshelves and earth shaking]
19.4	FX: BASA BASA BASA [books falling]
20-1.1	FX: BASA [book falling]
20-1.3	FX: BYOOOOOO [wind blowing]
22.1	FX: ELBO [whack]
22.2	FX: APPA [uppercut]
23.3	FX: KULULUN [twirl]
24.1	FX: DON [whump]
	FX: GOHO [coughing]
24.2	FX: DOSA [thud]
	FX: GEHO GEHO [coughing]
24.3	FX: BASHI [smack]
25.1	FX: GILI [gripping hard]
26.1	FX: BAKI [crack]
26.3	FX: FUWA [hair being lightly blown by a breeze]
26.4	FX: FUKI FUKI [wipe wipe]

64.1 FX: TOSA [whump]
64.2 FX: PASHI PASHI [flipping rock in palm]

65.1 FX: SUTO [landing lightly]
65.3 FX: GYU [squeeze]

66.2 FX: PON [pat]
66.3 FX: PA [quickly letting go]
66.5 FX: SUTA SUTA [stomp stomp]
66.6 FX: BITAN [thud]

67.2 FX: SUTA SUTA SUTA [stomp stomp stomp]
     FX: TATA [scamper]

69.1 FX: DA [dash]
     FX: BUTTOBI [boing]
69.4 FX: TATATA [running]

70.1 FX: GALA GALA [roll roll]
     FX: TATA [walking]

71.1 FX: SHU SHU [small objects being thrown fast]
71.2 FX: BON BON [smoke bombs going off]
71.3 FX: BA [whisking away]
71.4 FX: HIHIIIN [horse whinny]
     FX: GEHE GAHA [coughing]
     FX: SUTA [landing on the ground]
     FX: ZAWA ZAWA [crowd talking]

73.3 FX: POU [glow]
73.4 FX: GEHEGEHE GOHOGOHO [hacking, coughing]

74-5.1 FX: KAAAAAAAA [light emanating]
       FX: SUU [becoming transparent]
74-5.2 FX: SUU [becoming transparent]
74-5.4 FX: WAAAAAAH [crowd shouting]
       FX: KYAAAAA [woman screaming]

76.1 FX: SUUU [appearing]
76.2 FX: SUUU [appearing]
76.4 FX: HISHI [grasping tightly]
76.5 FX: SHIN [silence]

77.5 FX: JAKI [spears being pointed]

CHAPTER THREE:
THE PRIESTESS OF SUZAKU

80.1 FX: GYU [squeeze]
80.3 FX: ZAZA [backing away quickly]

82.3 FX: ZUKIN [stab at heart]
82.5 FX: PEN [slap]

84.2 FX: KASA [putting hand in skirt pocket]

85.4 FX: GASHI [grasp]

CHAPTER TWO:
THE BOY WITH THE DEMON STAR

49.3 FX: SHIN [silence]
49.4 FX: GALA GALA GALA GALA [clip clop clip clop]
49.5 FX: GABA [whoosh]

50.1 FX: GALA GALA GALA GALA [clip clop clip clop]
50.3 FX: ORO ORO [fluster fluster]

51.1 FX: GALA GALA GALA GALA [clip clop clip clop]
51.3 FX: GALA GALA [clop clop]
     FX: TON [feet hitting ground]

52.3 FX: ZOLO ZOLO [shuffle shuffle]

53.4 FX: JIRO JIRO [stare stare]

54.1 FX: GUKYULULULU [growling stomach]
54.3 FX: DAAAA [drooling profusely]
54.4 FX: CHALIN [money clinking]

55.1-4 FX: TA TA TA TA TA TA TA TA [skipping lightly]

56.1 FX: WAAA WAAA [crowd yelling, cheering]
56.2 FX: TEKU TEKU [walking dispiritedly]
56.3 FX: PON [tap]

57.5 FX: ZAWA ZAWA ZAWA [laughing, talking]

58.1 FX: PIKU [ping]
58.2 FX: POLI POLI [crunch crunch]
58.4 FX: SA [swish]
58.5 FX: NIKO [grin]

59.1 FX: SUTA SUTA SUTA SUTA [stomp stomp stomp stomp]
59.3 FX: PIKA [stop]

60.3 FX: PILA [flip]
60.4 FX: PAN [whack]
60.5 FX: JILI JILI [scratch scratch]

61.2 FX: BA [rolling up sleeve]
61.4 FX: DOKOO [whack]

62.1 FX: DOSHEE [shriek]
62.2 FX: DON [thwack]
62.3 FX: DOKA DOKA DOKA [kick kick kick]
62.4 FX: YORO [wobble]
     FX: Asia Kong is a pro wrestler in Japan.

63.1 FX: DOTA [thud]
63.2 FX: DAN [wham]
63.3 FX: BATA BATA [struggle struggle]
63.4 FX: SHU [swish]
63.5 FX: BISHI [smack]

114.2 FX: KYU [cuddle]

117.1 FX: SU [pulling shirt aside]

119.5 FX: POKI POKO [cracking knuckles]

120.1 FX: SU [getting into fighting position]
120.3 FX: DOKA GA BISHI [hitting, kicking]

121.1 FX: PITA [stopping suddenly]

123.5 FX: PIKU PIKU [twitch twitch]

124.1 FX: WANA WANA [tremble tremble]
124.2 FX: DON [very angry]
124.3 FX: BUN [punching]
       FX: HYOI [jumping out of the way]
124.4 FX: BAKI [breaking off]
       FX: SUTATATATA [scurry]
       FX: MEKI MEKI MEKI [crack crack crack]
124.5 FX: HAA HAA [pant, gasp]

125.1 FX: DON DOON [objects hitting columns]
125.2 FX: MEKI MEKI [crack crack]

126.2 FX: GALA GALA [crumble crumble]
126.4 FX: ZUDOON [structure imploding]
126.5 FX: PI PI [cha-ching]

127.4 FX: JIWA [blood soaking through skirt]

128.1 FX: ZUKIN [ouch]
128.4 FX: ZAWA ZAWA [murmur murmur]

129.3 FX: GIGIG [column pressing down]

130.2 FX: DOKUN [ba-dump]
130.3 FX: MIKI MIKI MIKI [crack crack crack]

131.3 FX: ZU [massive pressure]
131.4 FX: SU [moving quickly]

132.1 FX: GAKON [moving column]
       FX: HYOI [lifting]
132.2 FX: DOON [thud]
132.3 FX: PON PON PON [toss toss toss]
132.4 FX: GAKON [moving column]

134.2 FX: HELON [faint]
134.4 FX: NI [grin]

136.1 FX: NIKO [grin]

137.1 FX: SUI [whoosh]

CHAPTER FIVE: DANGEROUS LOVE

140.3 FX: BATAN [slam]

85.5 FX: GIII [creak]

86.1 FX: DOKI DOKI DOKI DOKI [ba-dump ba-dump ba-dump ba-dump]

87.4 FX: FULA FULA [stagger stagger]
87.5 FX: KULU [turn]

88.1 FX: SHIIIN [silence]
88.2 FX: FULA FULA [stagger stagger]

90.1 FX: GAAAAAAN [despair]

91.1 FX: NIKO [smile]
       FX: NIKO[smile]
91.3 FX: SUTA SUTA SUTA [stomp stomp stomp]
       FX: SUTO [landing lightly]
91.4 FX: NIKKORI [grin]

93.1 FX: HA [gasp]

94.3 FX: SALA [twinkle]
       FX: DOKI [ba-dump]

95.1 FX: HA [gasp]
95.4 FX: GA [whack]
95.5 FX: ZA [rushing out of bushes]

96.3 FX: GA [grab]
96.4 FX: DOGA [thwack]
96.5 FX: DOSA [konk]

97.1 FX: SU [symbol appearing on forehead]

98.1 FX: ZAZA [soldiers saluting]

101.5 FX: DOKUN DOKUN DOKUN DOKUN [ba-dump ba-dump ba-dump ba-dump]

103.3 FX: ZAWA [murmuring]

104.2 FX: ZA [bowing]

106.2 FX: KACHA KACHA [jiggling doorknob]
       FX: KOTSU KOTSU [shuffle shuffle]
106.5 FX: PALA PALA [flip flip]

107.2 FX: PATAN [whud]
107.4 FX: HETA [slump]

CHAPTER FOUR:
THE SEVEN CONSTELLATIONS OF SUZAKU

109.1 FX: PAPAAA [car horns beeping]
109.2 FX: HA HA [huff huff]
109.3 FX: TATA [running]

112.4 FX: KON [thonk]

164.5   FX: PAN [smack]

166.2   FX: DOKI [ba-dump]
166.3   FX: HYOI [lowering head]

167.4   FX: GUI [tug]

CHAPTER SIX: HIDDEN LOVE

170.1-2 FX: DOKUN DOKUN DOKUN DOKUN
        DOKUN DOKUN DOKUN DOKUN
        [ba-dump ba-dump ba-dump ba-dump
        ba-dump ba-dump ba-dump ba-dump]

171.1   FX: DOKIN [ba-dump]
171.4   FX: SU [moving quickly and quietly]

172.1   FX: SUTA SUTA SUTA [walking briskly]
172.2   FX: SU [drawing sword]
172.3   FX: HYU HYU HYU HYU [slice slice slice
        slice]
172.4   FX: PISHI PISHI [crack crack]
172.5   FX: BALA BALA [crumble]

173.6   FX: SUI [pang]

174.1   FX: PATA PATA [pitter patter]
174.2   FX: SU [grab]

176.4   FX: SU [walking by]

177.2   FX: SUTA SUTA [stomp stomp]
177.5   FX: ZUOOOOO [anger]

178.1   FX: ZUGOGOGOGO [anger]

179.4   FX: TON [stepping onto platform]

181.4   FX: GUI [whack]

182.2   FX: SHIIIIIN [silence]

184.1   FX: GYU GYU [squash squish]

187.1   FX: DOKI [ba-dump]
187.2   FX: DA [running]

188.2   FX: GUI [grab]
188.3   FX: GYO [shock]

192.1   FX: BAKI [thwack]
192.3   FX: DO [kick]

193.2   FX: ZAN [moving quickly]
193.3   FX: PI [snip]
193.4   FX: BAKI [thwack]
193.5   FX: DOSU [whud]

194.1   FX: SUTO [landing lightly on feet]

141.1   FX: JAAA [running water]
        FX: GOSHI GOSHI [scrub scrub]
141.2-3 FX: SU [stain vanishing]

142.2   FX: ZUKI [ouch]
142.5   FX: DOTATATA [stomp]

143.1   FX: BAM [slam]
143.3   FX: SHULULU [sash being flung]

144.2   FX: BATAN [slam]
        FX: HOHOHOHO [ha ha ha ha]

146.1   FX: HYOI [lifting hair]
146.2   FX: BISHA [splash]
146.6   FX: GAN [gonk]

148.1   FX: GAN [gonk]
148.2   FX: GYUU GYULULUUU [stomach growl-
        ing]

150.2   FX: GUI [yank]
150.4   FX: DOKIN [ba-dump]

151.3   FX: JI [stare]
151.4   FX: PUPU [heh heh]

156.2   FX: ZA [wind rustling through trees]
156.3   FX: HYOKO HYOKO [limp limp]

157.1   FX: BULU [shiver]
        FX: HYOKO [limp]
157.2   FX: BASA BASA [birds flapping wings]
157.3   FX: SHULU [tendril whipping out]
        FX: ZAZA [drag]
157.4   FX: ZU [yank]

158.1   FX: PATAN [door closing quietly]
158.2   FX: BISHU [splash]
158.3   FX: POTA POTA [drip drip]

159.3   FX: GABO GABO GABO [gurgling under-
        water]
        FX: GOBO [coughing underwater]
159.4   FX: JIWA [bandages loosening]

160.3   FX: TOTATATA [running]
160.4   FX: ZA [turn]

161.1   FX: BAN [wham]
161.2   FX: GUI [yank]
161.5   FX: BUCHI [snap]

162.2   FX: GA [grab]
162.5   FX: GYUU [clutch]

163.2   FX: POTA POTA [drip drip]
163.3   FX: HYOKO HYOKO [hobble hobble]

164.4   FX: PAN [smack]

GET THE COMPLETE
FUSHIGI YÛGI COLLECTION

What happens when the hottest guy in school is a girl?!?

Find out in the popular manga series!

With original artwork by series creator Hisaya Nakajo, your favorite characters come to life in this art book!

Hana-Kimi™